Dazzling Science Projects with Light and Color

Robert Gardner

Enslow Elementary

an imprint of

E **Enslow Publishers, Inc.**

40 Industrial Road   PO Box 38
Box 398   Aldershot
Berkeley Heights, NJ 07922   Hants GU12 6BP
USA   UK

http://www.enslow.com

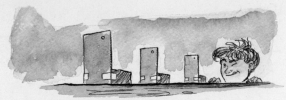

Enslow Elementary, an imprint of Enslow Publishers, Inc.

Enslow Elementary® is a registered trademark of Enslow Publishers, Inc.

Library of Congress Cataloging-in-Publication Data

Gardner, Robert, 1929–
    Dazzling science projects with light and color / Robert Gardner.
       p. cm. — (Fantastic physical science experiments)
    Includes bibliographical references and index.
    ISBN-10: 0-7660-2587-X (hardcover)
    1. Light—Experiments—Juvenile literature.
    2. Spectrum analysis—Juvenile literature. I. Title.
    QC360.G3665 2006
    535—dc22
                                                       2005009498

ISBN-13: 978-0-7660-2587-5

Printed in the United States of America

10 9 8 7 6 5 4 3 2

To Our Readers: We have done our best to make sure all Internet Addresses
in this book were active and appropriate when we went to press. However, the
author and the publisher have no control over and assume no liability for the
material available on those Internet sites or on other Web sites they may link to.
Any comments or suggestions can be sent by e-mail to comments@enslow.com
or to the address on the back cover.

Illustration credits: Tom LaBaff

Cover illustration: Tom LaBaff

Contents

(Experiments with a 🎖 symbol feature **Ideas for Your Science Fair**.)

Introduction

This book is filled with experiments about light and color. Doing experiments will help you learn about light—a form of energy that moves very fast. How does light travel? Does light ever bend? How does light help you see? Can you mix light of different colors? Can you make colored shadows? You can answer these questions by doing the experiments in this book.

Entering a Science Fair

Most of the experiments in this book (those marked with a 🎗 symbol) are followed by ideas for science fair projects. However, judges at science fairs like experiments that are creative. So do not simply copy an experiment from this book. Expand on one of the ideas suggested, or think of a project of your own. Choose a topic you really like and want to know more about. Then your project will be more interesting to you. Your curiosity can lead to a creative experiment that you plan and carry out.

Before entering a science fair, read one or more of the books listed under Further Reading. They will give you helpful hints and lots of useful information about science fairs.

Safety First

To do experiments safely, always follow these rules:

❶ Do experiments under adult supervision.

❷ Read all instructions carefully. If you have questions, check with the adult.

❸ Be serious when experimenting. Fooling around can be dangerous to you and to others.

❹ Keep the area where you work clean and organized. When you have finished, clean up and put materials away.

❺ Never experiment with electric wall outlets.

❻ Never look directly at the sun.

1. Light's Path

Things you will need:
- ✔ three 3-in x 5-in file cards
- ✔ paper punch
- ✔ tape
- ✔ 3 wooden blocks
- ✔ yardstick, meterstick, or ruler
- ✔ a friend
- ✔ flashlight
- ✔ sheet of white paper
- ✔ thin string

❶ Hold three file cards with their edges together. Use a paper punch to make holes in all three cards at the same time. Each hole will be at the same place on each card.

❷ Tape each card to a wooden block. The bottom edge of each card should touch the bottom edge of its block (see the drawing).

❸ Place the cards about 20 inches (50 cm) apart on a table or counter near a window. Look through the hole farthest from the window. Move the second card until you see light through both holes. Have a friend move the third card until you see light through all three holes.

4 Darken the room. Shine a flashlight straight through the hole you looked through. You should see a circle of light on a paper held beyond the third hole.

5 Cut a piece of thin string about two yards (two meters) long. Thread the string through all three holes. Be careful not to move the cards. Have your friend hold one end of the string while you hold the other. Carefully tighten the string. Do the holes lie along a straight line? What does this tell you about the path followed by light?

3-in x 5-in file card   **wood block**

Light's Path:

You put a string through all three holes and pulled it tight. All the holes were along a straight line. You could see a narrow beam of light from a window through the same three holes. Light from a flashlight also passed through all three holes and fell on a sheet of paper. To get through all three holes, the light must have traveled along a straight line.

Light travels in straight lines as long as it stays in one substance, such as air or water. When it passes into a different substance, it usually bends, as you will see in Experiment 4.

Because light travels in straight lines, it makes shadows. Light that hits an object cannot go through it. The object blocks the light. This makes it darker on the side away from the light. We call the dark area a shadow. You have probably seen your shadow on a sunny day. You can also see your shadow in a room at night. Just turn on a light!

An Explanation

Idea for Your Science Fair

★ Design and do other experiments to show that light travels in straight lines in air and in water.

2. Light and Seeing

Some people used to think they could see things because light came out of their eyes and bounced off objects. You can test this idea.

Let's Begin!

Things you will need:
- ✔ closet
- ✔ a friend
- ✔ towel (optional)
- ✔ flashlight
- ✔ small mirror
- ✔ table
- ✔ room that can be darkened
- ✔ clay

1 Read instructions 2 and 3. Then continue.

2 Take a flashlight into a closet with a friend. Face your friend. Close the door so that the closet is totally dark. If light is leaking in the bottom of the door, cover the area with a towel. Do you see light coming from your friend's eyes?

3 After a few seconds, turn on the flashlight. Shine it about for a while. Then open the door.

What could you see when you turned on the flashlight? Why do you think the flashlight let you see things? What kinds of light do you normally use to see things?

4 Stand a small mirror upright on a table in a dark room. You may need to support the mirror with clay.

5 Shine a flashlight on the mirror (see the drawing). Look for light on a wall in front of or next to the mirror. How can you show that the light on the wall is bouncing off the mirror?

6 Shine light on the mirror at different angles by moving the flashlight from side to side. How does changing the angle affect light bouncing off the mirror?

mirror

flashlight shining on mirror at bigger angle

Light and Seeing:

The closet remained dark until you turned on the flashlight. Light did not come out of your friend's eyes!

Light from the flashlight bounced off (reflected from) objects and entered your eyes. You could see things on which the flashlight shone. Light moves away from its source. Sources of light include the sun, lightbulbs, candles, fires, and light sticks (chemicals that glow). When light strikes an object, some of it bounces off (reflects) and travels to your eyes.

You can prove the light on the wall came from the mirror. Face the mirror, with your eye in front of the light on the wall. You will see the flashlight in the mirror. Or, hold a piece of paper against the light on the wall. Move the paper toward the mirror, keeping the light's path on the paper. You will see that the light comes from the mirror.

When you shine light on a mirror, it bounces off (reflects from) the mirror. Make the angle at which the light hits the mirror bigger (see the drawing). The angle at which the reflected light leaves the mirror

An Explanation

will also get bigger. In fact, light is reflected at the same angle at which it strikes the mirror.

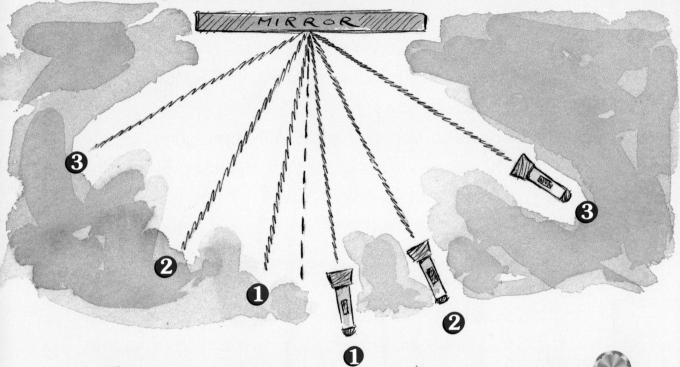

Ideas for Your Science Fair

* By doing an experiment, show that the angle at which light strikes a mirror equals the angle at which it leaves the mirror.
* "If I can see you in a mirror, you can see me!" Design experiments to show why this statement is true.

3. Transparent, Translucent,

Light can pass right through some objects. Such objects are called transparent.

Other things block light. Light cannot pass through them. These objects may reflect light, absorb light, or do both. Such objects are called opaque. They can cast dark shadows.

Translucent things are in between. They allow some light to pass through them. But they scatter or absorb the rest of the light. You cannot see clearly through translucent materials.

Let's Begin!

❶ Gather a number of items such as a drinking glass, cardboard, water in a clear glass, waxed paper, aluminum foil, plastic wrap, a sheet of white paper, tissue paper, a mirror, a frosted lightbulb, and other handy materials.

❷ Test each item by holding it in front of a clear lightbulb, a window, or a flashlight.

❸ Classify each object. Is it transparent, opaque, or translucent? How would you classify your eyelids? Your hands?

or Opaque?

Things you will need:
- ✔ drinking glass
- ✔ cardboard
- ✔ water
- ✔ waxed paper
- ✔ aluminum foil
- ✔ plastic wrap
- ✔ many sheets of white paper
- ✔ tissue paper
- ✔ mirror
- ✔ frosted lightbulb
- ✔ other items
- ✔ clear lightbulb, bright window, or a flashlight
- ✔ colored glass

4 Test a stack of white paper. How does the stack compare with one sheet of paper?

5 Look through a piece of colored glass. How would you classify the colored glass?

paper

waxed paper

water

cardboard

Transparent, Translucent,

You most likely classified the items you tested like this:

Item	Class
glass	transparent
cardboard	opaque
water	transparent (if shallow)
waxed paper	translucent
mirror	opaque
eyelids	translucent
frosted bulb	translucent
white paper	translucent
tissue paper	translucent
aluminum foil	opaque
plastic wrap	transparent
hand	opaque

One sheet of paper is translucent. A stack of many sheets is opaque. This tells you that each sheet absorbs (soaks up) some light. When light has to pass through many sheets, all the light is absorbed.

Deep-sea divers know it is dark deep below the ocean's surface. Just as paper absorbs some light, so does water. As light passes through a lot of water, a little bit of light is absorbed at a time. After a while, very little light is left. In the ocean, sunlight passes only through the top layers of water. It is very dark deep in the ocean.

or Opaque: An Explanation

If you look through a piece of green glass, everything looks green. The glass takes out (absorbs) other colors. Only green light comes through the glass. This shows that ordinary light (white light) contains light of many colors. You can explore that idea in Experiment 6.

green glass

4. Bending Light

What happens to light when it goes from one transparent substance to another? You can do an experiment to find out.

Let's Begin!

Things you will need:
- ✓ long pencil
- ✓ glass of water
- ✓ penny
- ✓ a friend
- ✓ teacup
- ✓ milk
- ✓ eyedropper
- ✓ measuring cup
- ✓ small, clear, plastic or glass jar with a flat bottom
- ✓ white paper
- ✓ table
- ✓ dark room
- ✓ comb
- ✓ flashlight

① Put a long pencil in a glass of water. Look at the pencil from the side. What do you notice?

② Put a penny on the bottom of a teacup. Lower your head until the coin just disappears from view. Hold your head there. **Do not move!** Have a friend slowly pour water into the cup. Why do you think the coin becomes visible? What must happen when light passes from water to air or vice versa?

③ Pour a cup of water into a clear jar. Add 10 to 12 drops of milk to the water and stir. Place the jar on a sheet of white paper resting on a table.

4 In a dark room, hold a comb in front of the jar. Shine a flashlight through the comb into the jar. What happens to the narrow beams of light as they enter and leave the jar? This experiment will help you explain the convex lens you will use in the next experiment.

jar with milky water

Bending Light:

When you looked at the pencil, it seemed to be broken. Why? Because light usually bends when it goes from one clear substance to another. For example, it bends when it goes from air to glass, glass to water, water to plastic, and so on. When the light from the pencil went from water to air, the light bent.

You saw the penny when water was added to the teacup. Light from the penny bent when it went from water to air. Now you know that things are not always where they appear to be.

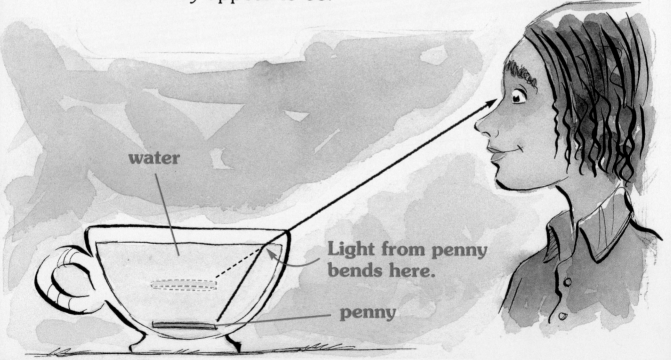

water

Light from penny
bends here.

penny

An Explanation

The experiment with the comb also showed that light bends. The comb created narrow beams of light. The beams of light bent as they entered and left the water.

The jar of water is like the lens in a camera. When light enters and leaves a lens, it bends. We say the light is refracted. The bigger the angle at which light hits the lens, the more it is refracted. Light striking the edges of a lens bends more than light hitting its center. Lenses have a particular shape. With the right shape, a lens can bring light from every point on an object back together to form an image.

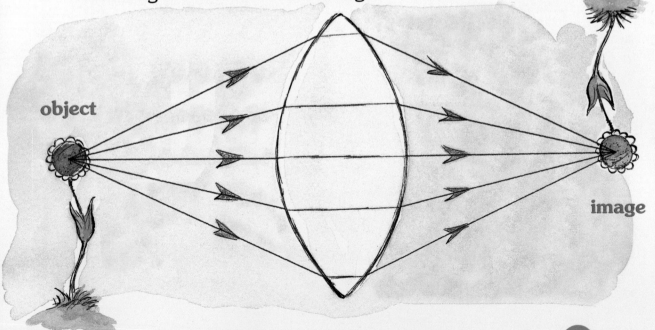

object

image

5. Light, Lenses, and Eyes

What happens to light that enters your eye? How does the light let you see?

Look at your eyes in a mirror. Look closely at the colored part (the iris). See the small black circle in the middle of the iris? It is called the pupil. The pupil is a small opening that lets light into your eye. Behind the pupil and iris is a lens. You can't see the lens, but you can do an experiment to find out what the lens does to light entering your eye.

Let's Begin!

1. Find a magnifying glass. It is a lens like the lens inside your eye.

2. Hold the lens near a white wall opposite a window that lets in light from outside. Move the lens back and forth. At one position of the lens you will see a clear "picture" (image) on the wall. The lens makes an image of what you see through the window. What do you notice about the image? Is it colored? Is it right side up? What must your eye's lens do to light to make the images you see?

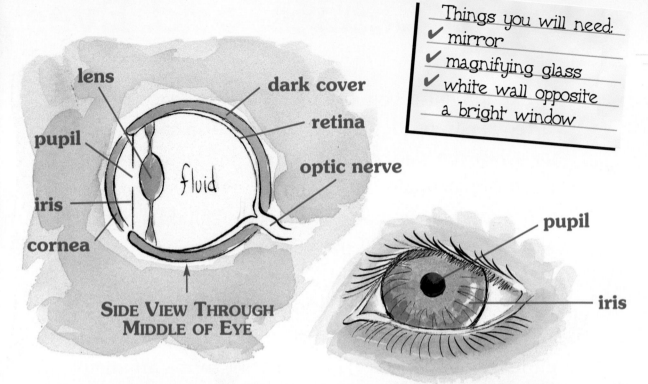

lens

dark cover

pupil

retina

optic nerve

fluid

iris

cornea

SIDE VIEW THROUGH MIDDLE OF EYE

pupil

iris

Things you will need:
✔ mirror
✔ magnifying glass
✔ white wall opposite
a bright window

Light, Lenses, and Eyes:

In Experiment 2 you saw that mirrors reflect light in a regular way. Light is reflected at the same angle that it hits the mirror. Calm water and other smooth surfaces reflect light the same way. But most surfaces are not smooth, so they do not reflect light in a regular way. Light bounces off them in all directions.

In Experiments 4 and 5 you saw how a lens, like the one in your eye or a camera, brings light together. Light coming in all directions from an object is bent (refracted) by the lens. The bent light forms an image or picture of the object. The image is upside down because of the way the lens bends light (see the drawing).

In your eye, the image forms on the back of your eye. The retina, which is on the back of your eye, has many tiny cells. When light hits these cells, they send signals to the brain. In your brain, you see these signals as an image. Your brain has learned to see the images as being right side up.

An Explanation

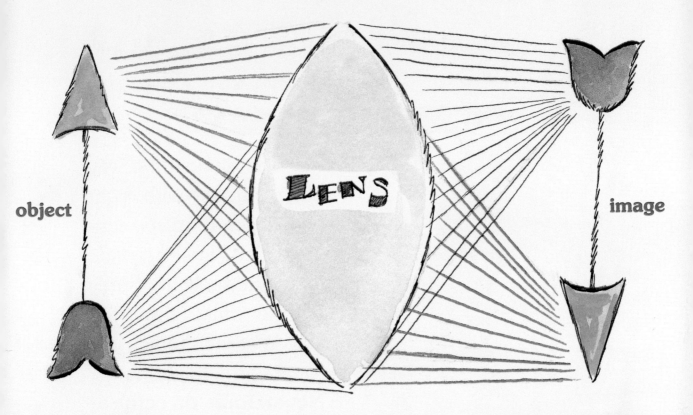

object

image

LENS

Ideas for Your Science Fair

★ What happens when light passes through a *concave* lens?

★ How does the lens in your *eye* differ from a rigid glass or plastic lens? Make a model to show how the lens in a human *eye* works.

★ Show how eyeglasses help a person see.

A rainbow shows that light can be separated into colors.

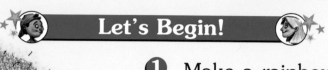

Let's Begin!

1 Make a rainbow the way nature does—with light and water droplets. Use a garden hose outside in bright sunlight. Spray a fine mist into the air. Where should you stand to see the rainbow? **Never look directly at the sun. It can hurt your eyes.**

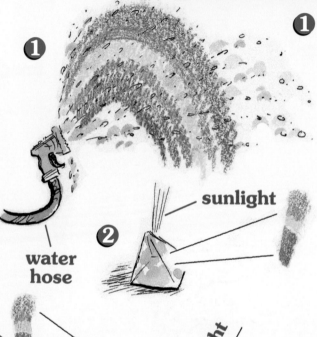

water hose

sunlight

sunlight

2 Hold a prism between sunlight and a wall. Turn it until you see a "rainbow" on the wall.

3 Place a dishpan of clean water in sunlight near a wall. Put a hand mirror in the water. Look for a rainbow on the wall. Or move a piece of white cardboard several

Many Colors

feet from the mirror until you "catch" a rainbow. An overhead incandescent lightbulb can be used in place of the sun.

④ Using scissors, cut a very narrow slit about 2 inches long in a file card. Fold the card. Put it in front of a prism or a clear, rectangular plastic container filled with water. Shine a flashlight through the slit. The narrow beam of light should hit the prism or water at a small angle (see the drawing). A rainbow will appear beyond the prism or container. Which color is bent the most?

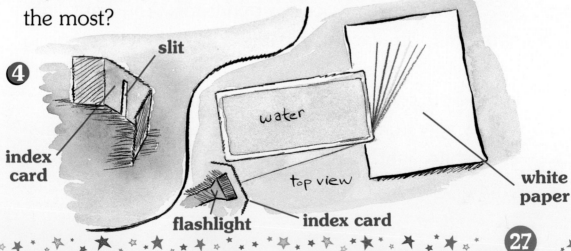

slit

④

index card

water

top view

flashlight   index card

white paper

Light Contains Many

To see a rainbow, the sun must be behind you. To find out why, you need to know how a rainbow is made. Raindrops are like tiny lenses. Sunlight entering a raindrop is bent (refracted) as shown in the drawing. As you see, violet light bends more than red light. Some of the bent light is reflected inside the raindrops. The reflected light bends again as it leaves the raindrop. Your eyes receive red light from higher drops and violet light from lower drops. That is why you see red at the top of a rainbow and violet at the bottom.

Water, glass, and plastic all bend violet light more than red light. Violet light appears to be "pushed" off its path more than red light. In between are blue, green, yellow, and orange. These colors are separated into a spectrum (a rainbow of colors).

Light is bent twice by raindrops. You bent light two times in each experiment you did. Refracting light twice makes a better spectrum because the colors spread out more each time the light is bent.

A spectrum can be made by bending (refracting) any white light. It does not have to be sunlight. An ordinary incandescent bulb will do.

Colors: An Explanation

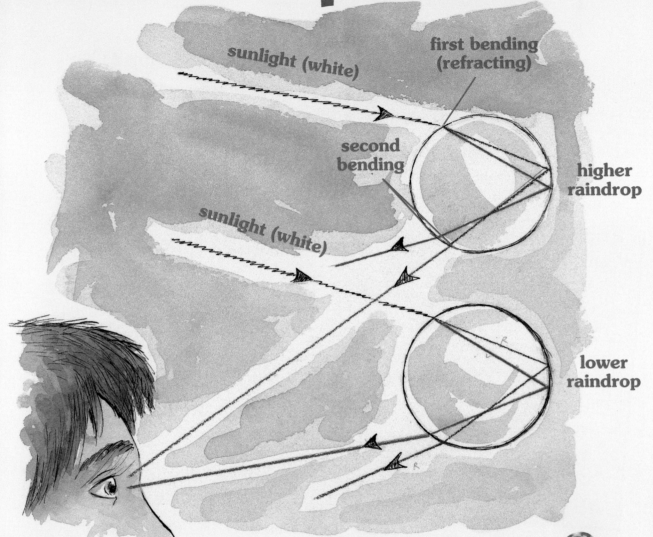

sunlight (white)

first bending (refracting)

second bending

higher raindrop

sunlight (white)

lower raindrop

Idea for Your Science Fair

★ The colored lights separated by a prism can be put back together to make white light. Can you find a way to do it?

7. Mixing Colored Lights

What happens when you mix colored lights? Can colors found in a rainbow make white light? Have **an adult** help you experiment to find out.

Let's Begin!

Things you will need:
- ✔ an adult
- ✔ 3 light sockets
- ✔ red, blue, and green lightbulbs (25-watt)—purchase at a supermarket or hardware store
- ✔ white wall
- ✔ dark room
- ✔ cardboard sheet about 11 in × 17 in

❶ Place light sockets with red, blue, and green lightbulbs near a white wall in a dark room. Have **an adult** plug in the lights.

❷ Turn on the red and blue lights. Hold a cardboard sheet between the two bulbs and against the wall. Pull the cardboard back several inches. This will let the two colors overlap (mix) on the wall. What color do you see when you mix blue and red lights?

❸ In the same way, mix blue and green lights. Then mix red and green lights. What color do you see when you mix blue and green? Red and green?

4 Turn on all three lights. Hold a cardboard sheet against the wall and between the red and blue bulbs (see the drawing). Pull the cardboard back a tiny bit so that the red and green lights can mix. Then pull it farther back so that all three colors can mix. What color do you see when you mix all three colored lights? What colors did you mix to make white light?

6 in

Mixing Colored Lights:

The colors you saw when you mixed colored lights may have surprised you. They are not the colors you get when you mix paints. Blue light plus red light makes a color called magenta. You might call it pink. Blue light plus green light makes a color called cyan. You might call it blue-green or aqua. Mixing red light and green light makes yellow.

With all three lights on, you put the cardboard against the wall between the red and blue bulbs. You saw red on one side of the cardboard and cyan (blue-green) on the other side. (Remember, the two bulbs on the other side of the cardboard were blue and green.) Mixing blue and green produces cyan. When you pulled the cardboard back just a small amount, you saw a thin yellow band. This is where the green and red lights overlapped. Pulling the cardboard back farther allowed all three lights to mix, producing white. The colors red, blue, and green combined to form white light. For that reason, they are called the primary colors of light.

An Explanation

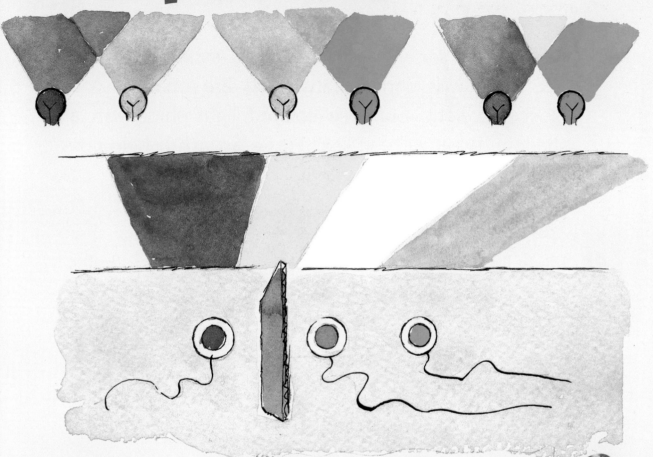

Ideas for Your Science Fair

★ Look at the light from colored and ordinary lightbulbs through a diffraction grating. What can you conclude?

★ Use a diffraction grating to look at the light that comes through colored glass or plastic. What can you conclude?

8. Colored Shadows

You can see your shadow on a sunny day. The shadow is dark because you are opaque; you block the light. Suppose colored light shines on a shadow. What will you see? **Have an adult** help you do an experiment to find out.

Let's Begin!

❶ Place light sockets with red, blue, and green lightbulbs near a white wall in a dark room. **Have an adult** plug in the lights.

❷ Turn on the blue light. Hold a pencil close to the wall in front of the light. Is the pencil's shadow dark? Is it dark if you use the red light? If you use the green light?

❸ Hold a pencil close to the wall. Predict how many shadows you will see when you turn on two colored bulbs. Turn on both the green and blue bulbs. Was your prediction correct? Can you explain the colored shadows you see?

❹ Repeat the experiment using red and green bulbs. How many shadows do you see? Can you explain the shadows' colors?

❺ Repeat the experiment using the red and blue bulbs. How many shadows do you see? Can you explain the shadows' colors?

❻ Repeat the experiment with all three bulbs turned on. How many shadows do you see? Can you explain the shadows' colors?

Things you will need:
✔ an adult
✔ the 3 light sockets and bulbs from Experiment 7
✔ white wall
✔ dark room
✔ pencil

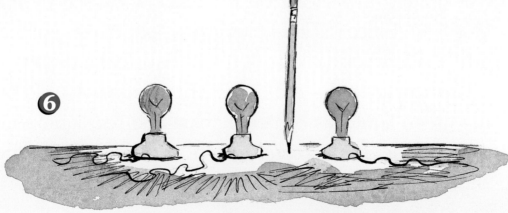

How many shadows will you see?

Colored Shadows:

An opaque object in any light casts a dark shadow. The shadow is dark because little or no light shines on it.

Two lights shining on an object will cast two shadows (A). The blue light and the green light each made a shadow of the pencil. Green light shone on the shadow caused by the blue light, so that shadow was green. Because blue light shone on the shadow caused by the green light, that shadow was blue. For the same reason, red and green shadows appeared when those two lights were on (B). And that is why you saw a red and a blue shadow when those two lights were on (C).

With three lights, there were three shadows (D). Their colors probably surprised you. Two lights, red and green, now shone on the shadow caused by the blue light. Since red light plus green light makes yellow, that shadow was yellow. (It might have been orange if it was closer to the red light.) The shadow caused by the green light was lighted by blue and red light, so it was magenta. Blue and green light shone on the shadow caused by the red light, so it was cyan.

An Explanation

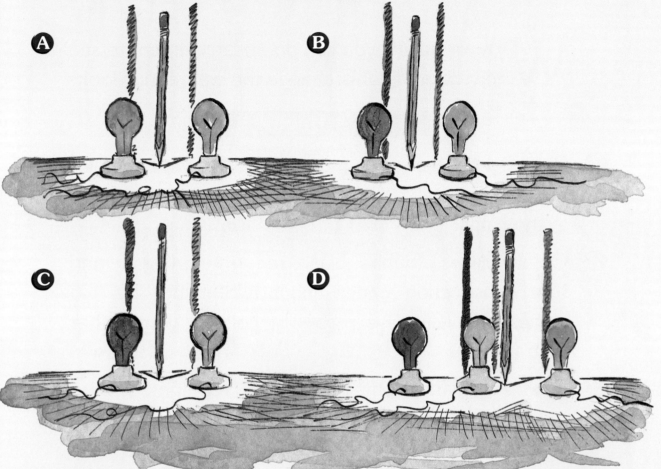

Idea for Your Science Fair

★ Look for colored shadows in the world around you and try to explain them. For example, shadows seen on snow are often blue. Shadows around a Christmas tree that has multicolored bulbs may have many colors.

9. Colors in Colored Light

With **an adult**, you can do an experiment to see how colored lights change the way things look.

Let's Begin!

1. Place light sockets with red, blue, and green lightbulbs near a white wall in a dark room. Have **an adult** plug in the lights.

2. Obtain pieces of white, black, red, green, yellow, and blue construction paper about two inches by two inches. (You can use pieces of colored yarn rather than paper.)

3. In a really dark room, turn on the red light. Hold a piece of white paper in the red light. What color does it have in red light? Write down what you find on a piece of paper.

4. Repeat the experiment for pieces of black, red, green, yellow, and blue paper. Write down the color you see with each piece.

5. Turn off the red light. Turn on the blue light. Repeat the experiment again for each piece of colored paper. Write down your results.

6 Turn off the blue light. Turn on the green light. Repeat the experiment again for each piece of colored paper. Write down your results.

Things you will need:
- ✔ an adult
- ✔ the 3 light sockets and bulbs from Experiment 7
- ✔ white wall
- ✔ dark room
- ✔ white, black, red, green, yellow, and blue construction paper, or pieces of yarn of the same colors
- ✔ paper and pencil

Colors in Colored Light:

A red object is red because it reflects red light. The red dyes in a red object absorb (soak up) all colors except red. The same is true of blue and green objects. They reflect only blue or green light. They absorb light of all other colors. Yellow, as you learned in Experiment 7, is a mixture of green and red light. Yellow objects reflect both green and red light.

A white object reflects all light. If only red light shines on it, it will appear red. In blue light it will appear blue, and so on. A black object absorbs light of all colors, so it looks dark in any colored light.

Blue objects appear dark in red and green light because these objects absorb red and green light. The same is true of green objects in red and blue light. It is also true of red objects in blue and green light.

Your observations might be different. For example, the blue paper may have looked green in green light. This happens if the blue paper reflects some green light as well as blue. Any object that contains dyes other than its basic color will reflect some of those other colors.

An Explanation

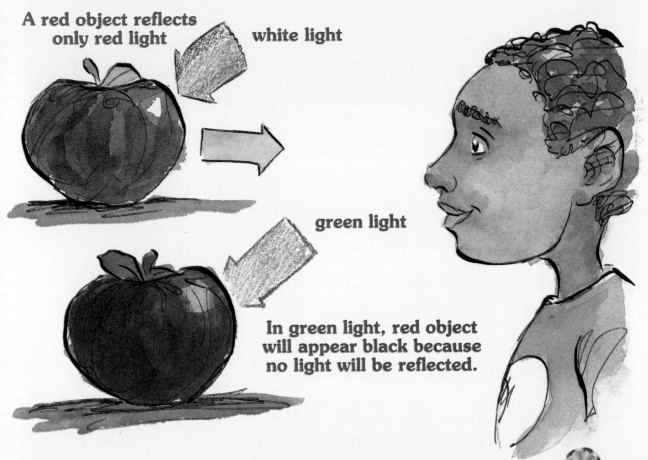

A red object reflects only red light

white light

green light

In green light, red object will appear black because no light will be reflected.

Idea for Your Science Fair

★ Obtain translucent pieces of plastic that have different colors. Predict what you will see when you look through a "sandwich" of different colors. To see what colors actually come through, look at the light with a diffraction grating in front of your eye.

10. Subtracting Color

An experiment can show that dyes soak up (absorb) colors from light. Use a diffraction grating. It separates light into the colors it contains.

Let's Begin!

1 Place a light socket on a table in a dark room. **Have an adult** screw a showcase bulb into the socket. **Have the adult** plug it in.

2 Stand several feet from the bulb. Hold a diffraction grating in front of your eye. Look to either side. You should see a spectrum (rainbow) of colors. They are the colors in the light from the bulb.

3 Put a drop or two of blue food coloring in a clear vial or small glass. Fill it with water. You should be able to see clearly through the colored water.

4 **Have the adult** hold the blue liquid in front of the bulb. Hold the diffraction grating in front of your eye. Look at the light coming through the blue liquid. What color or colors does the food coloring remove from the light?

5 Repeat the experiment using water colored by a drop or two of green food coloring. Repeat again using several

with Dyes

drops of red food coloring. Try again using several drops of yellow food coloring. What colors do these dyes remove from white light?

What part of the spectrum will the blue pigment remove?

Subtracting Color with

In Experiment 7 you added together lights of different colors. In this experiment you subtracted colors from white light. Dyes, like those found in food coloring, soak up (absorb) certain colors from light. They reflect other colors or let them pass through. You used a diffraction grating to look at white light that went through food coloring dissolved in water. The grating has many closely spaced slits. Light passing through the slits spreads out into a spectrum (rainbow) of colors. Any colors absorbed by the dye will not be in the spectrum.

You probably found that the blue food coloring removed most of the yellow, orange, and red parts of the spectrum. The green food coloring most likely removed everything except the green and some of the blue. The red food coloring probably removed most of the blue and green parts of the spectrum. And the yellow likely subtracted most of the blue end of the spectrum. The colors not absorbed by the food coloring remain in the spectrum. The colors that came

Dyes: An Explanation

through the liquid gave it the color you saw—blue, green, red, or yellow.

What colors are absorbed by the green, yellow, and red pigments?

Idea for Your Science Fair

★ Use a diffraction grating or a spectroscope to determine what colors come from neon signs and other colored lights.

Words to Know

diffraction grating—A device that has many slits very close together. It separates light into the colors the light contains.

dye—A chemical used to color material. It soaks up some colors from white light and reflects others.

lens—Glass, plastic, or other transparent material with curved sides that bend light.

light—A form of energy that we see with our eyes.

opaque substance—A substance that blocks light completely.

prism—A transparent, triangular solid object that bends light.

reflection—The "bouncing" of light from a smooth surface such as a mirror.

refraction—The bending of light as it passes from one transparent material to another.

spectroscope—A device containing a diffraction grating or a prism that spreads light out into a spectrum; it is used to show all the colors that are present in a beam of light.

spectrum—A range of colors produced by a light source.

translucent substance—A substance that allows some light to pass through it, but that scatters or soaks up the rest of it.

transparent substance—A substance that light can pass through, such as glass.

Further Reading

Books

Bombaugh, Ruth J. *Science Fair Success, Revised and Expanded.* Springfield, N.J.: Enslow Publishers, 1999.

Gold-Dworkin, Heidi, et al. *Exploring Light and Color.* New York: McGraw-Hill, 2000.

Hunter, Rebecca M. *Light and Dark.* Orlando, Fla.: Raintree Steck-Vaughn, 2000.

Lauw, Darlene, and Lim Cheng Puey. *Light.* New York: Crabtree Publishing Co., 2002.

Nankivell-Aston, Sally, and Dorothy Jackson. *Science Experiments with Light.* Danbury, Conn.: Franklin Watts, 2000.

Tocci, Salvatore. *Experiments with Light.* Danbury, Conn.: Children's Press, 2000.

Internet Addresses

The Exploratorium. *Exploratorium Science Snacks.* "Snacks About Light." n.d.

<http://www.exploratorium.edu/snacks/iconlight.html>

NASA. *Space Place.* "Why Is the Sky Blue?" March 17, 2005.

<http://spaceplace.jpl.nasa.gov/en/kids/misrsky/misr_sky.shtml>

Index